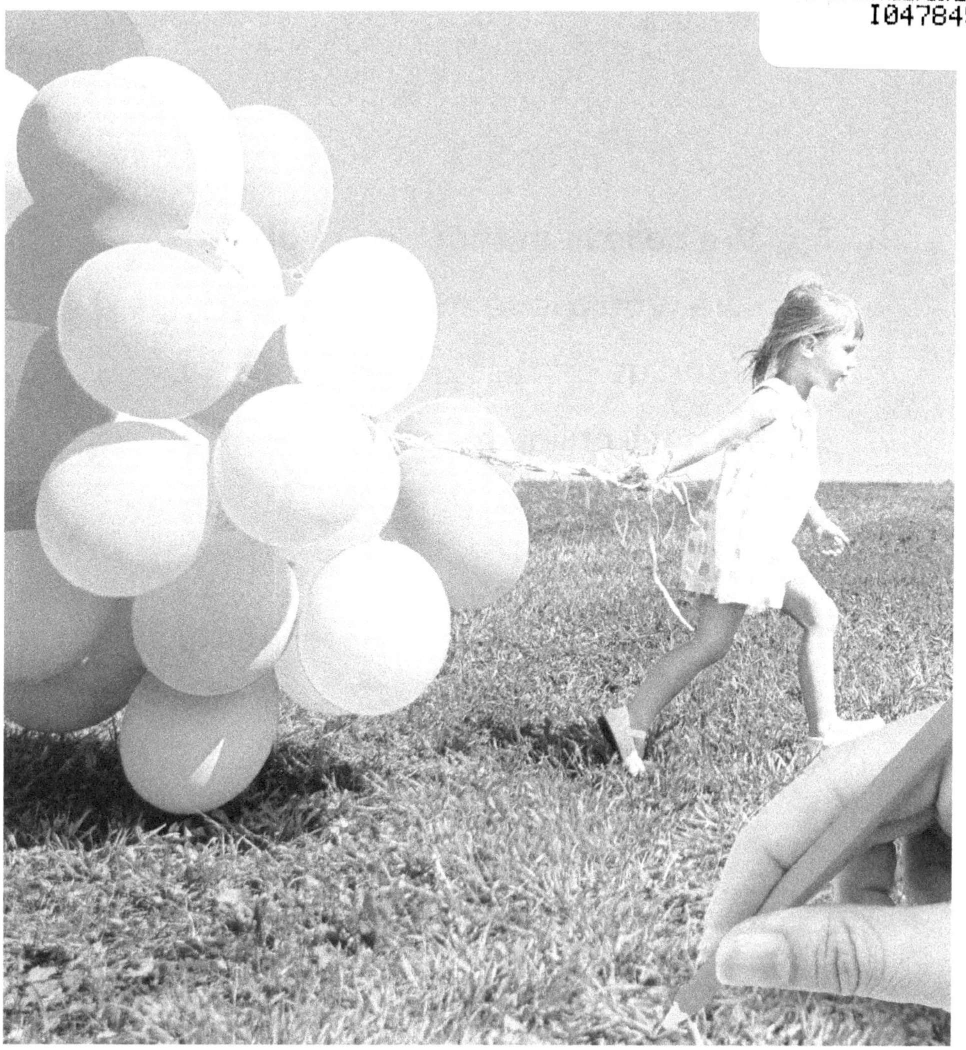

CUTE KIDS

We believe in sharing art and
we would love to see yours!
Send us or post your colored
pages online for all to love.

Facebook: fb.me/colormezenbooks

Instagram: ColorMeZenBooks

Twitter: #colormezenbooks

Find More Books: www.ColorMeZen.com

COLORED PENCIL
for coloring light/medium areas

CRAYON
for texture or adding some dark outlines

MARKER
for solid areas or coloring bright outlines

INK
for adding very dark outlines or dark sketching

PASTELS
for adding light or vivid bright coloring

GRAPHITE
for creating shading or to darken lines

WATERCOLOR
for light painterly colors or effects

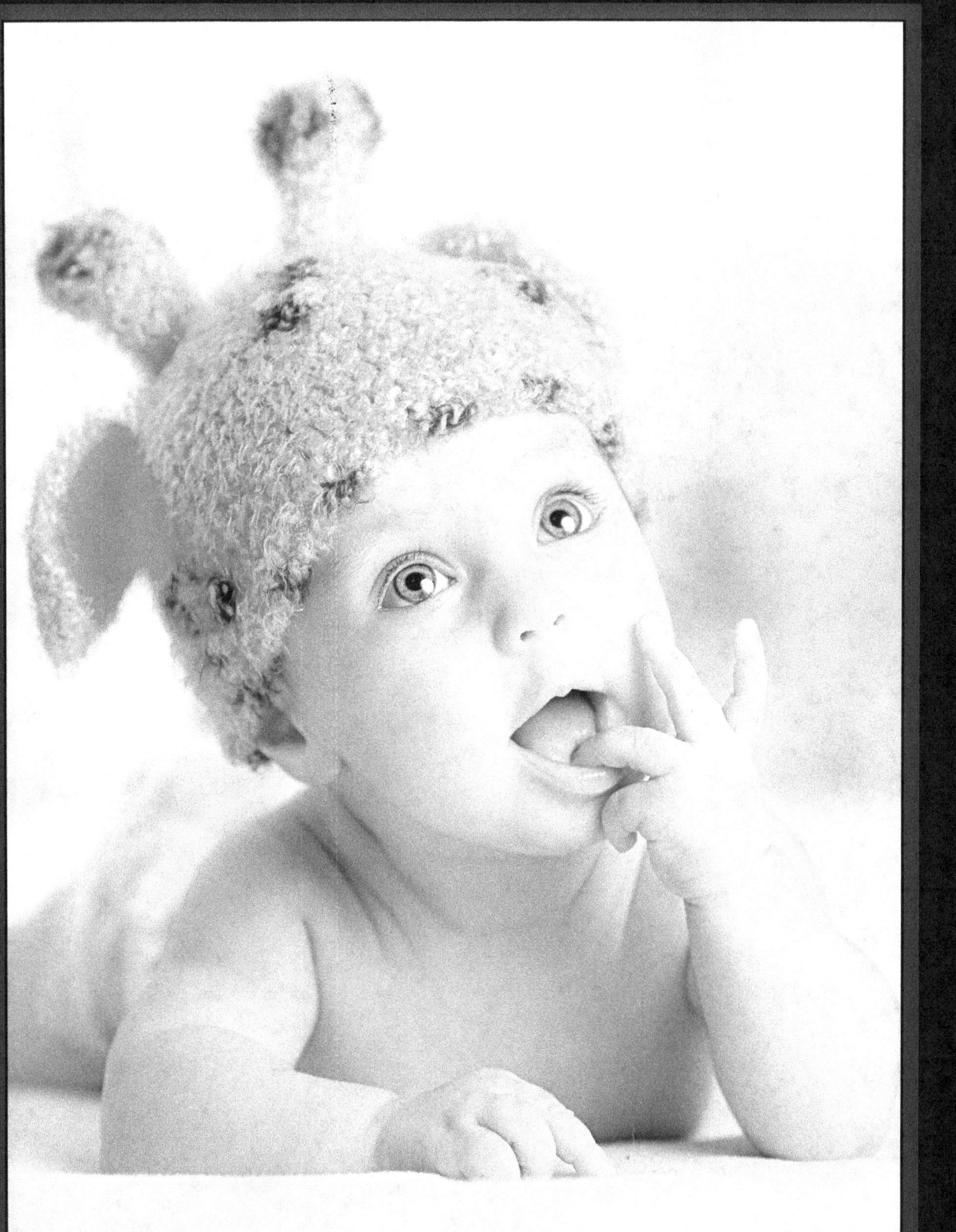

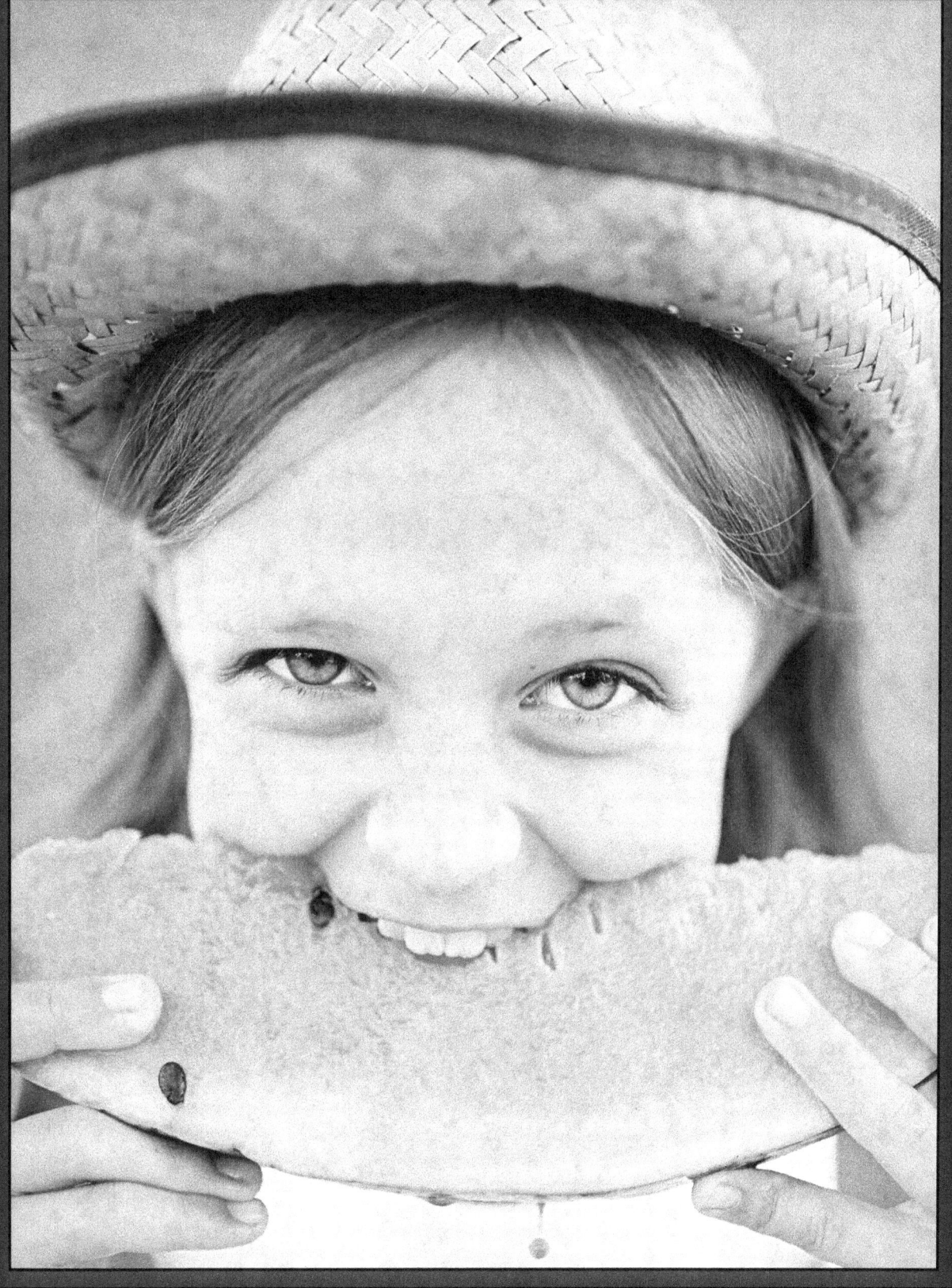

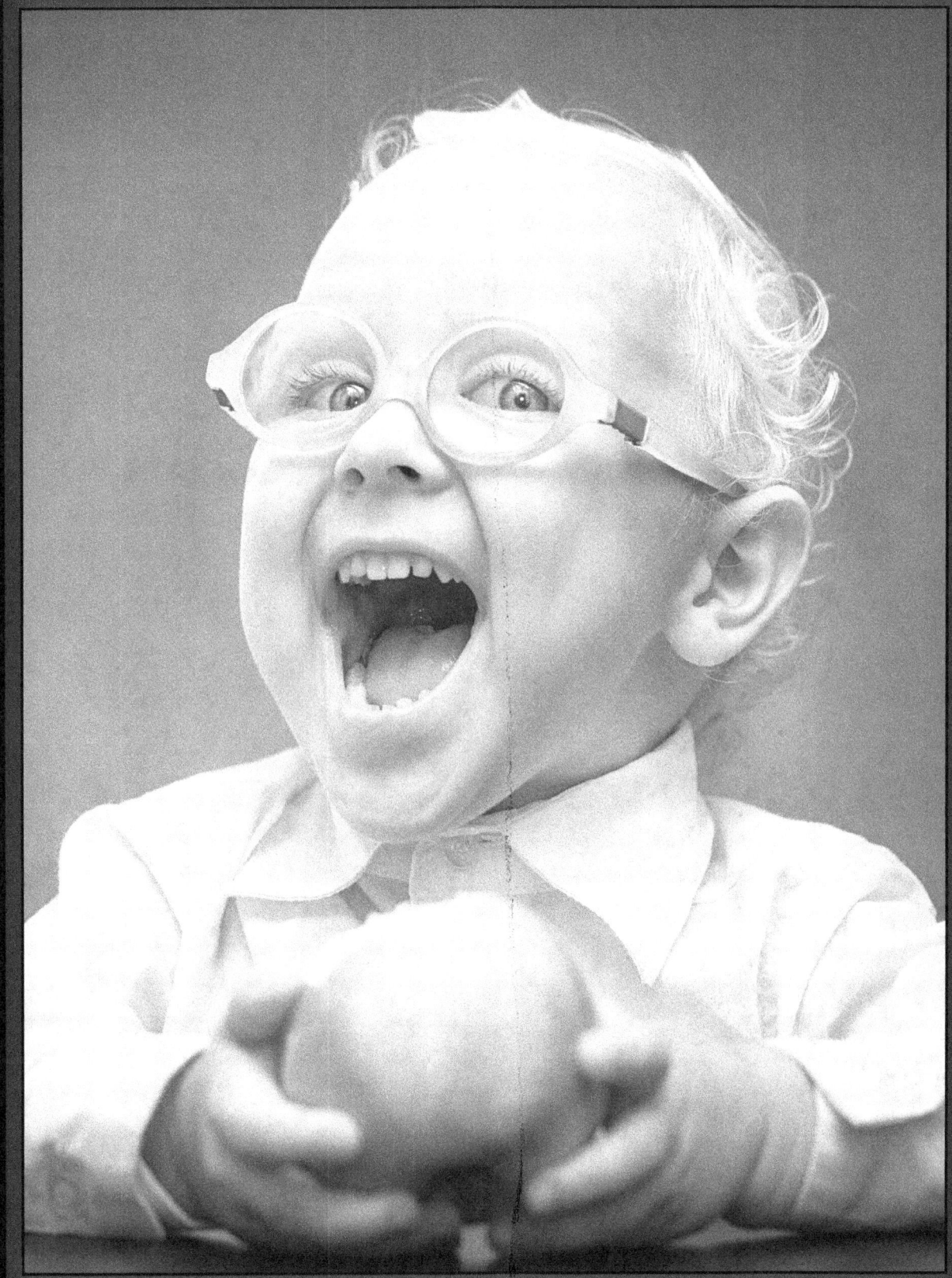

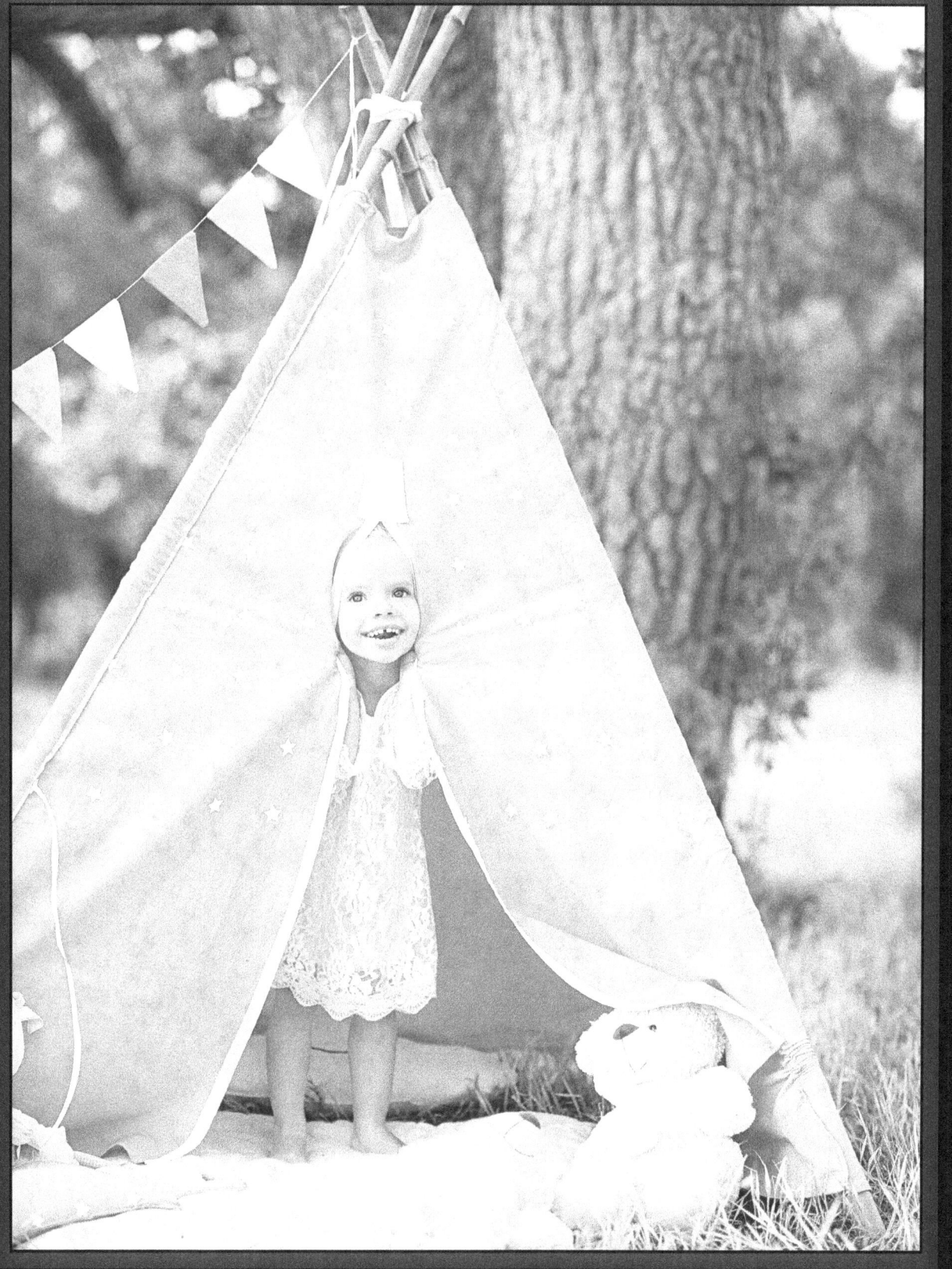

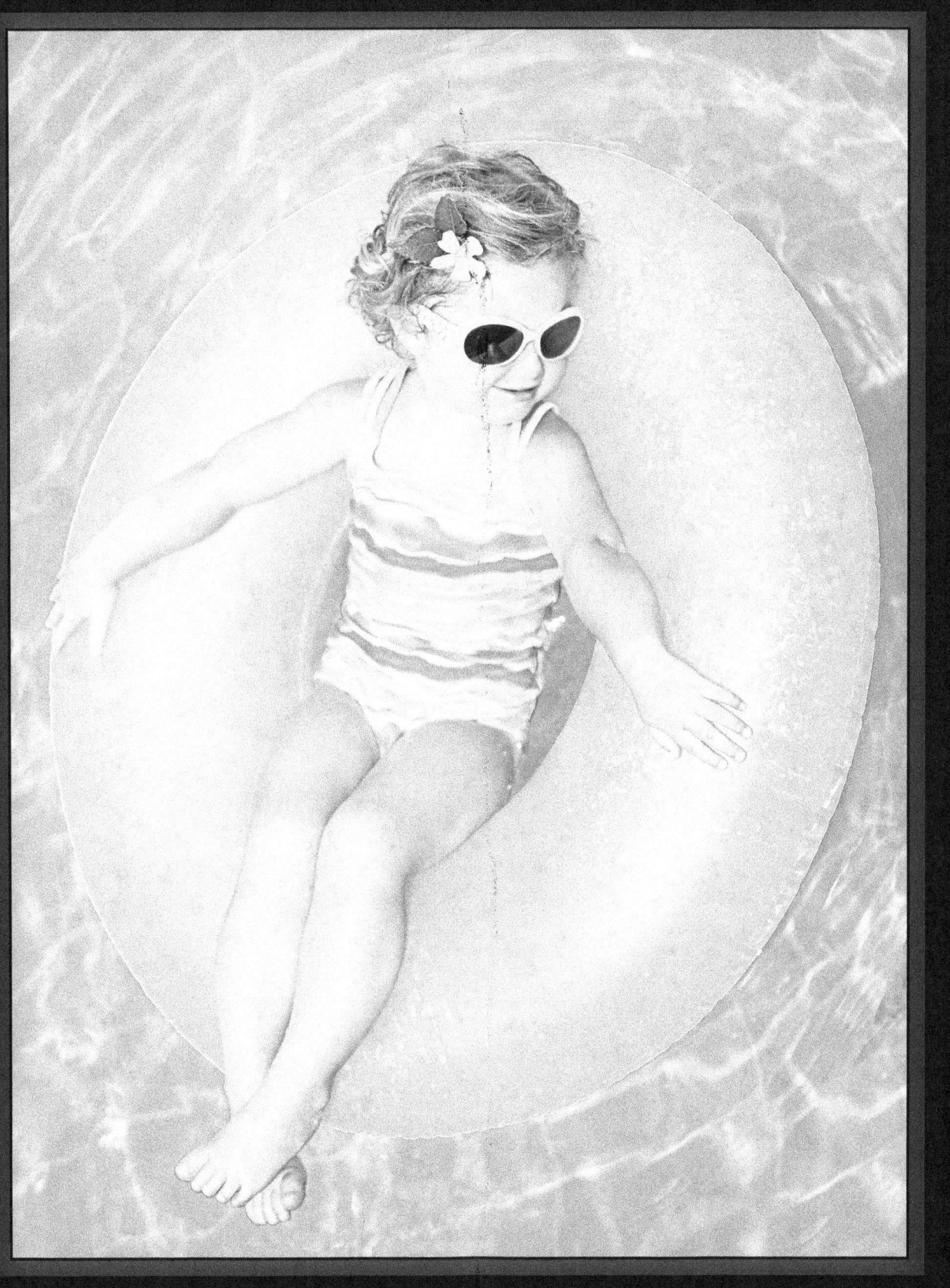

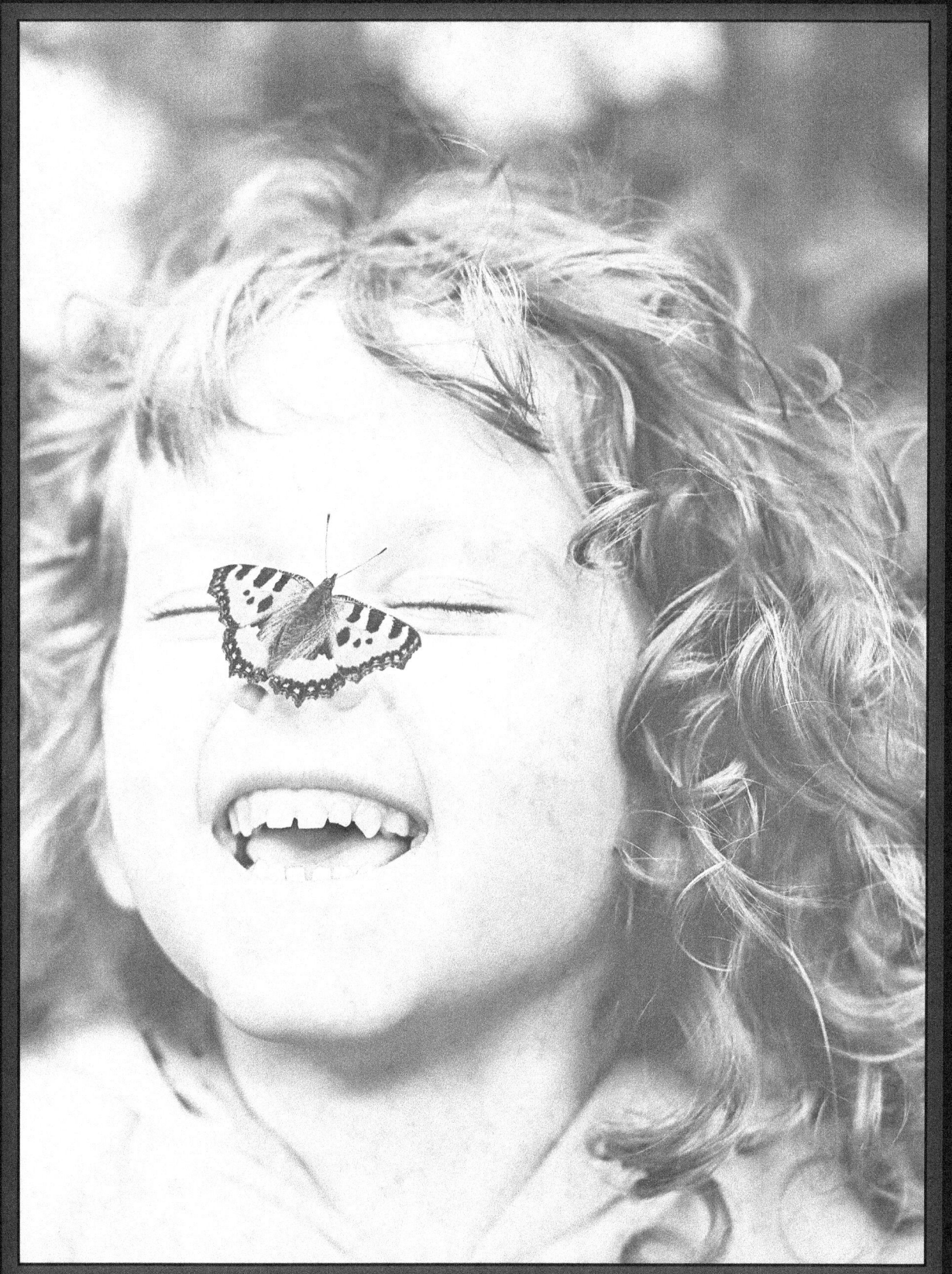

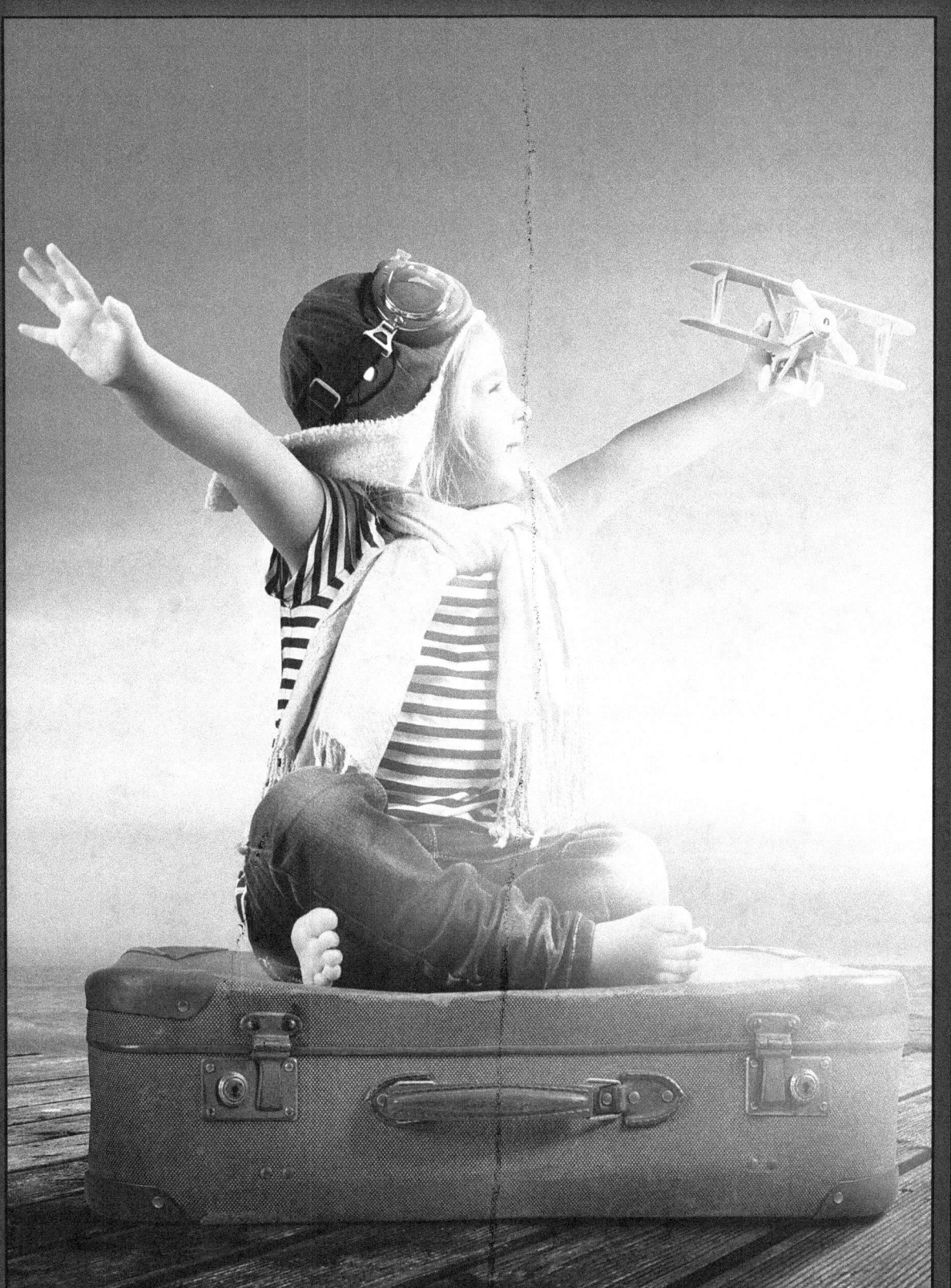

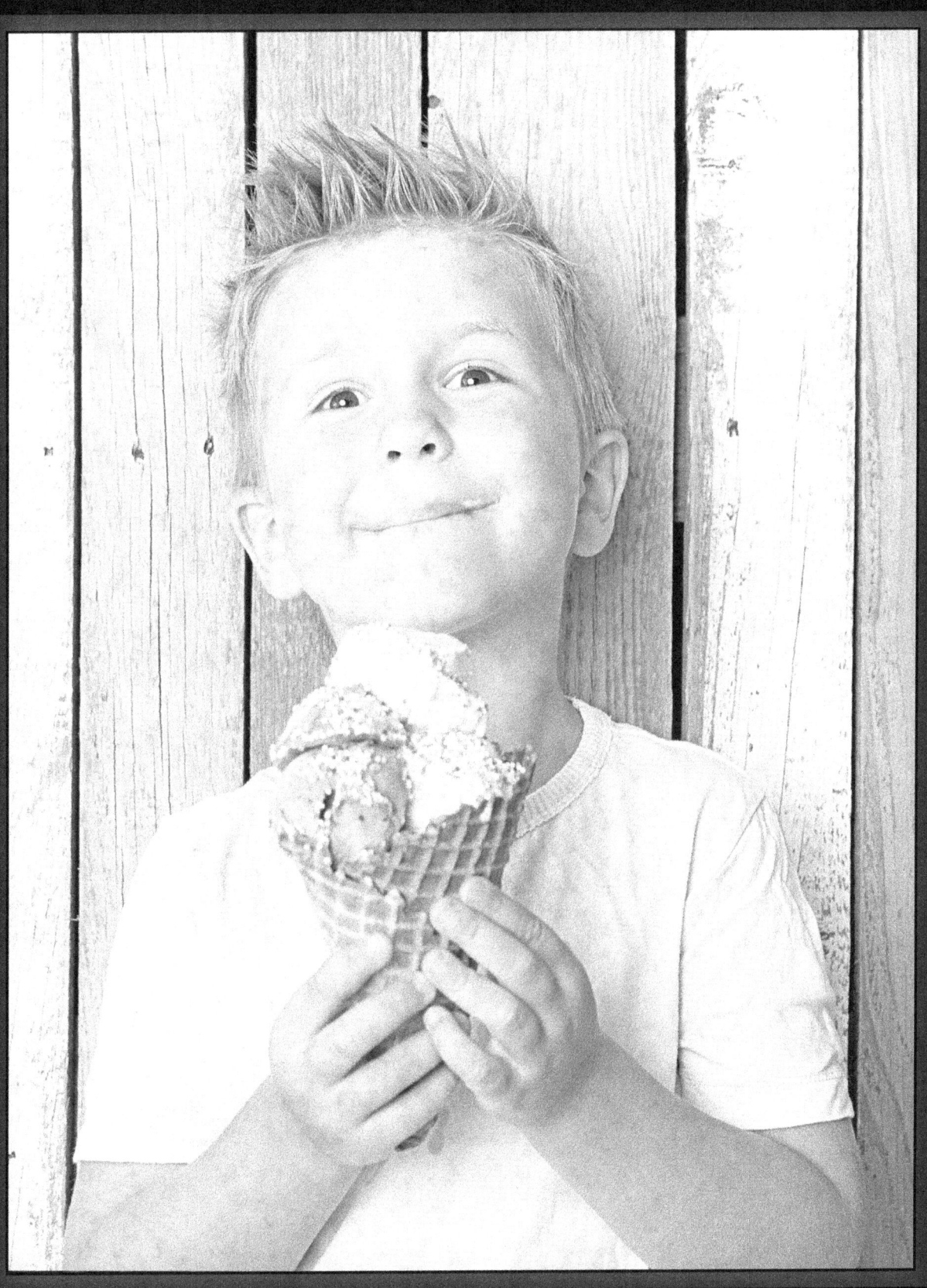

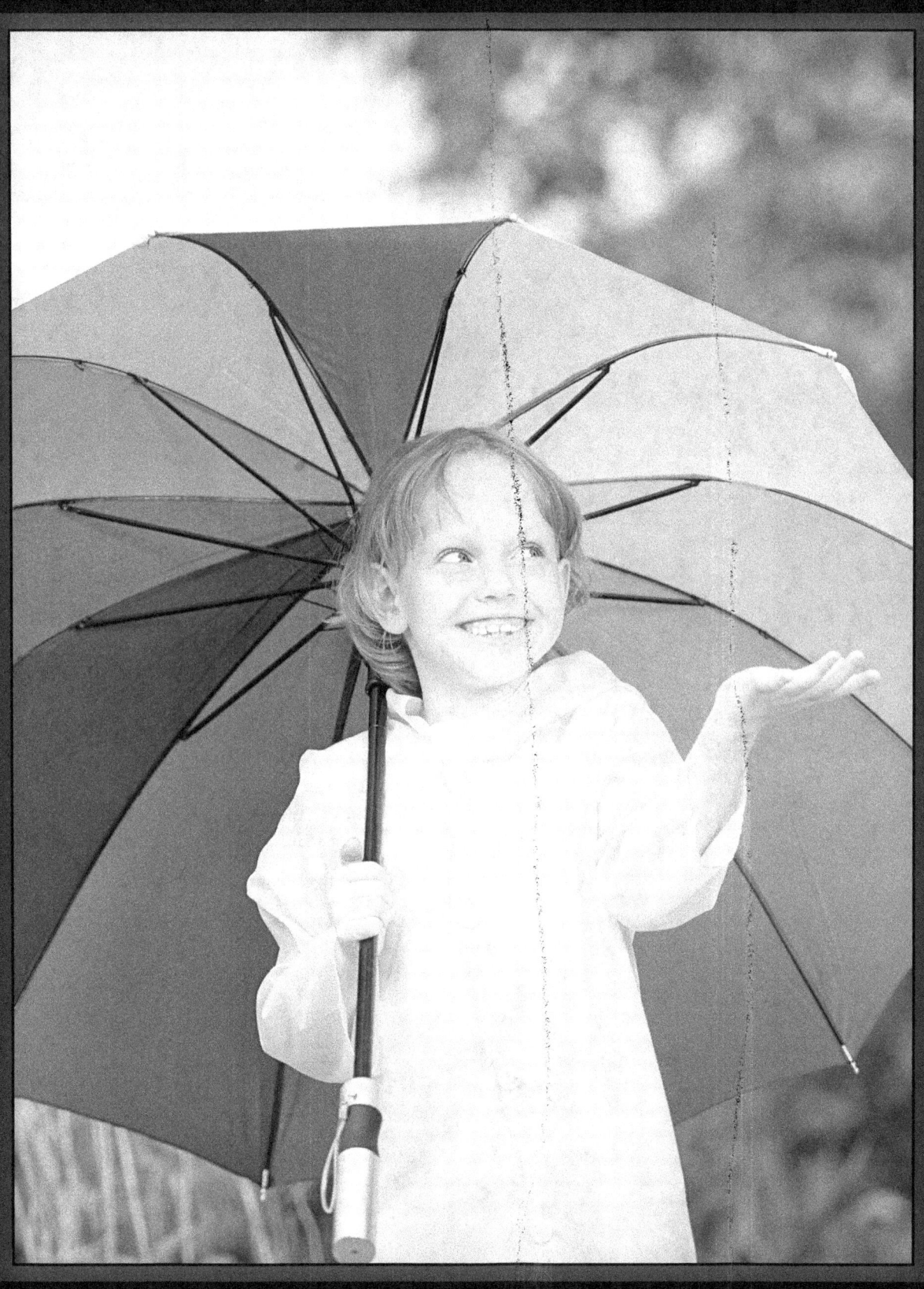

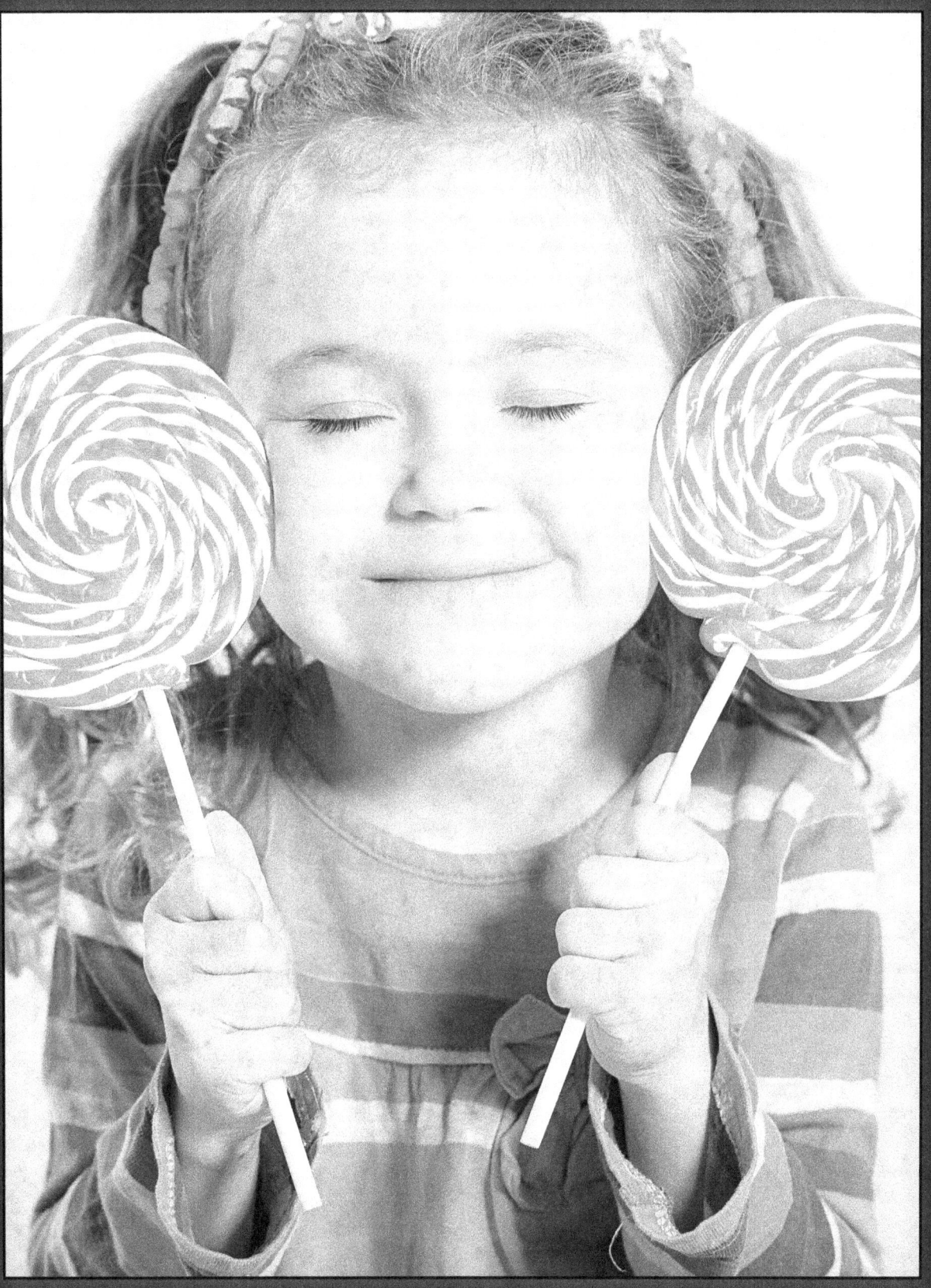

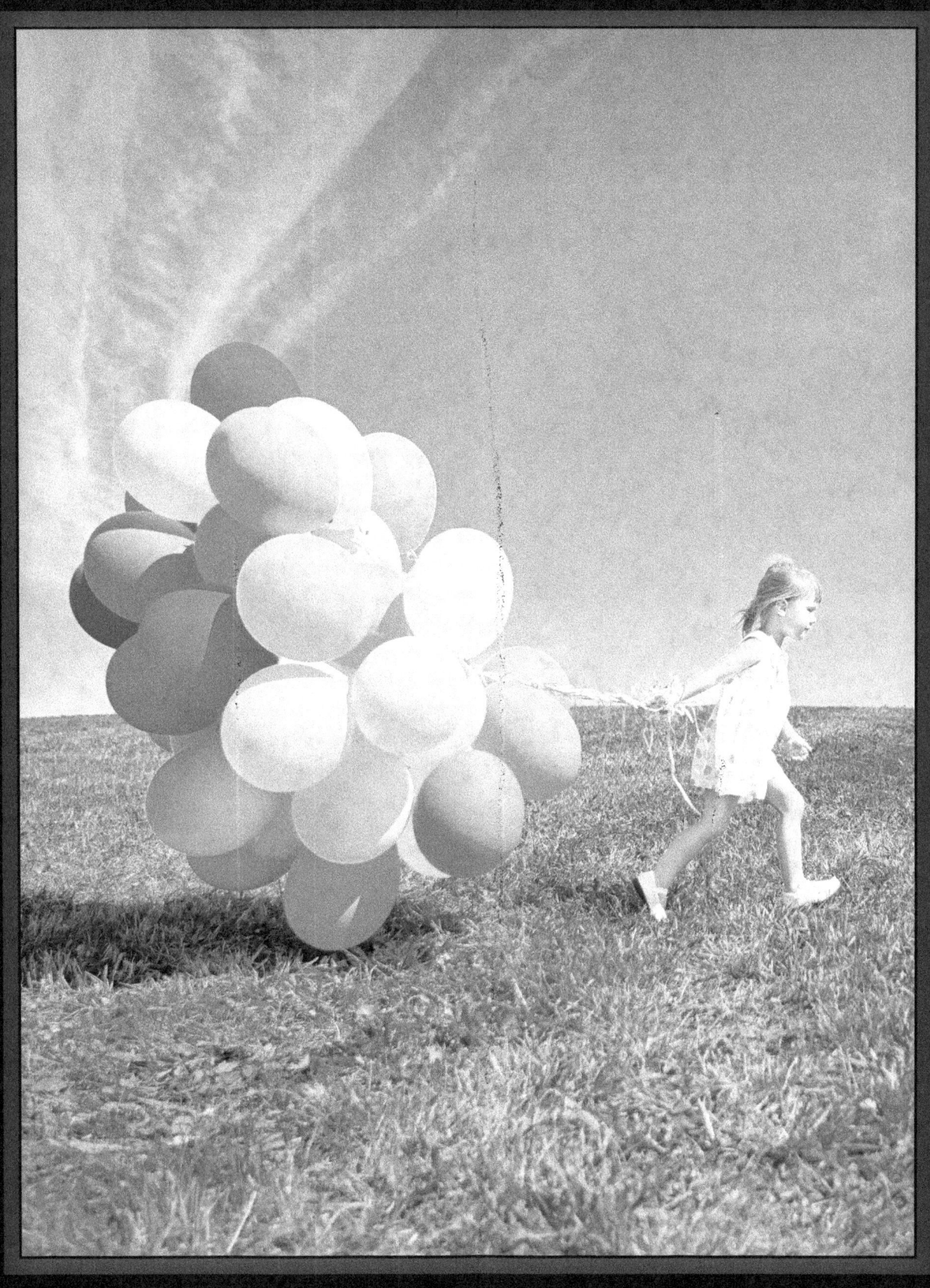

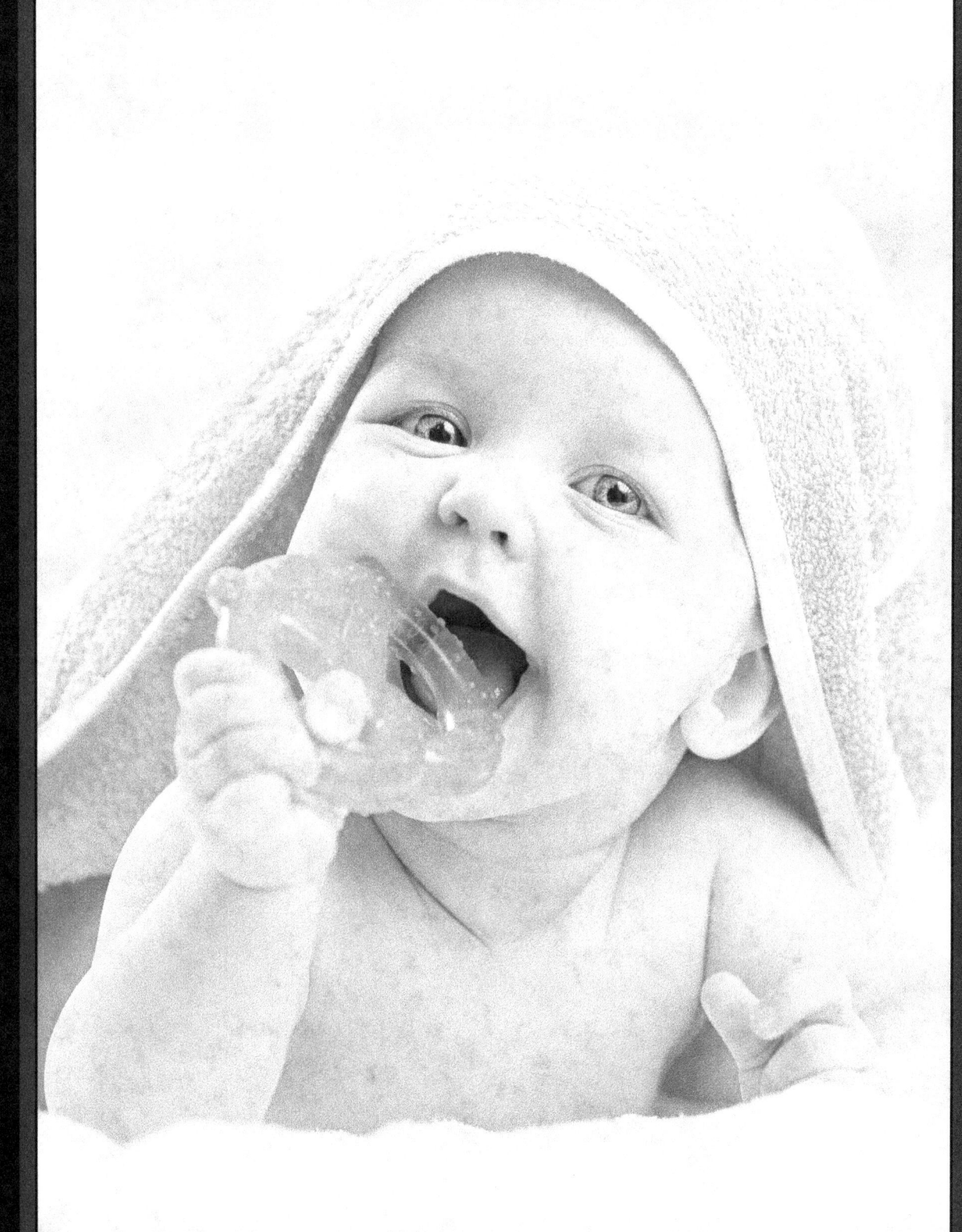

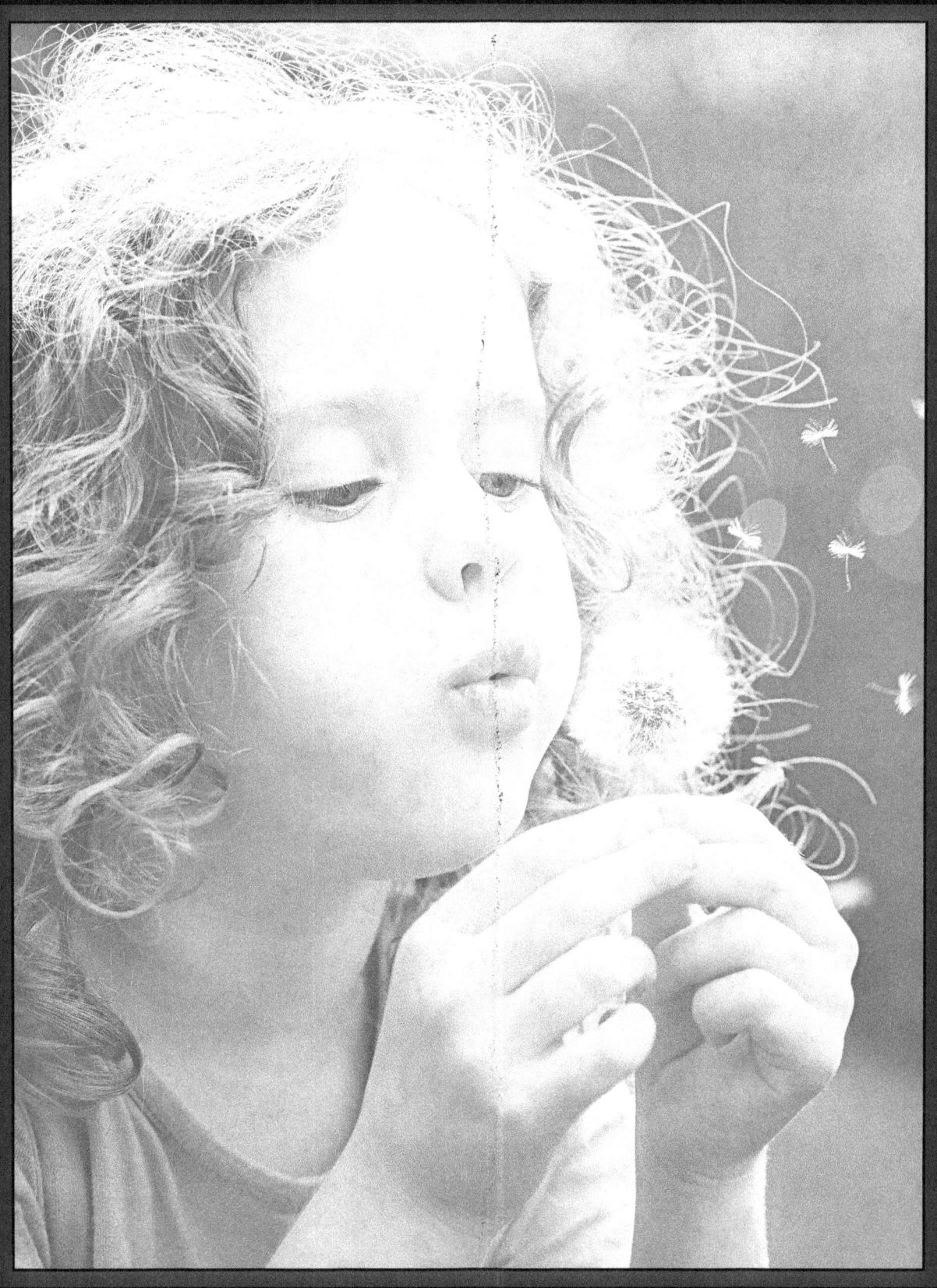

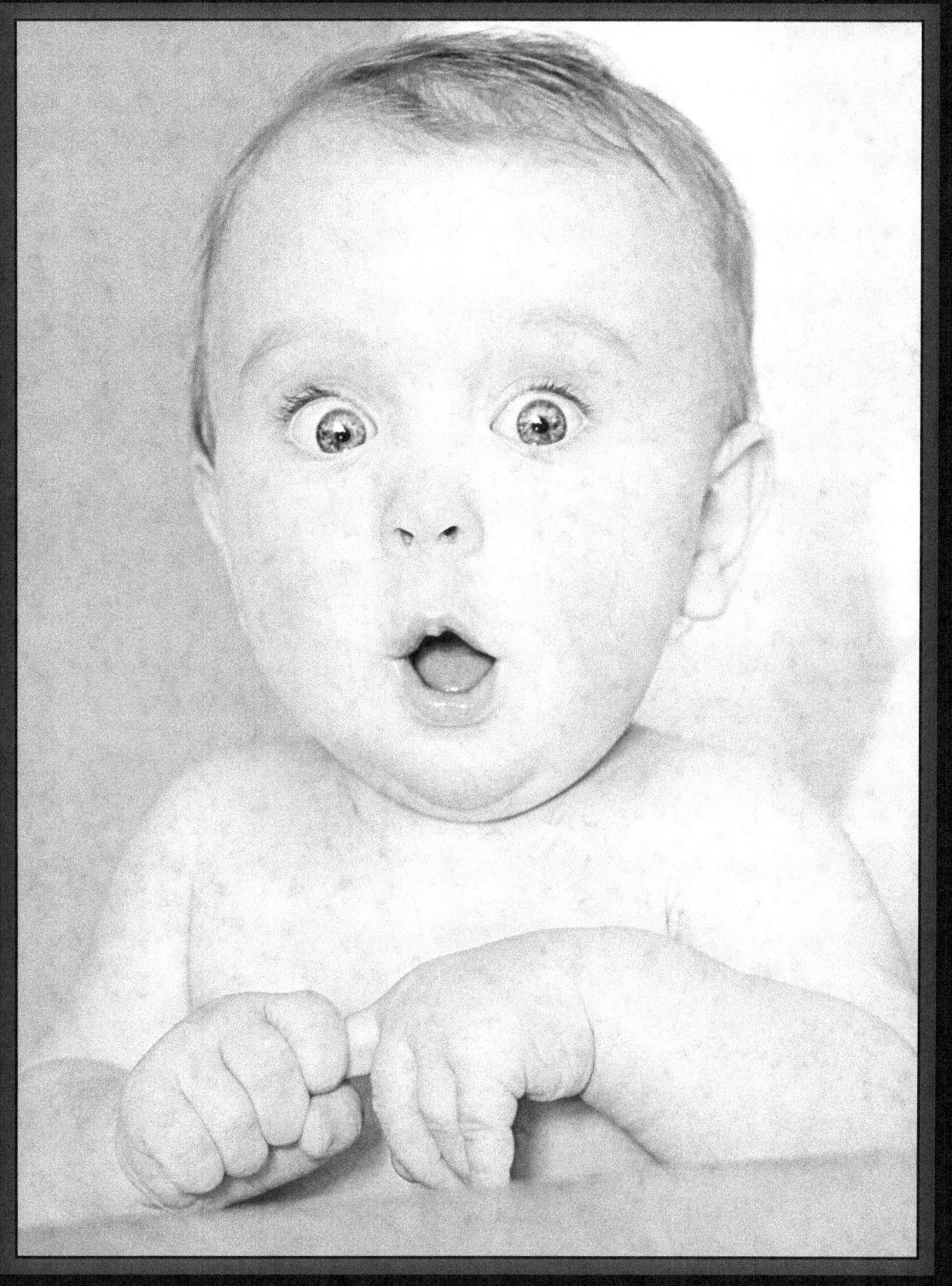

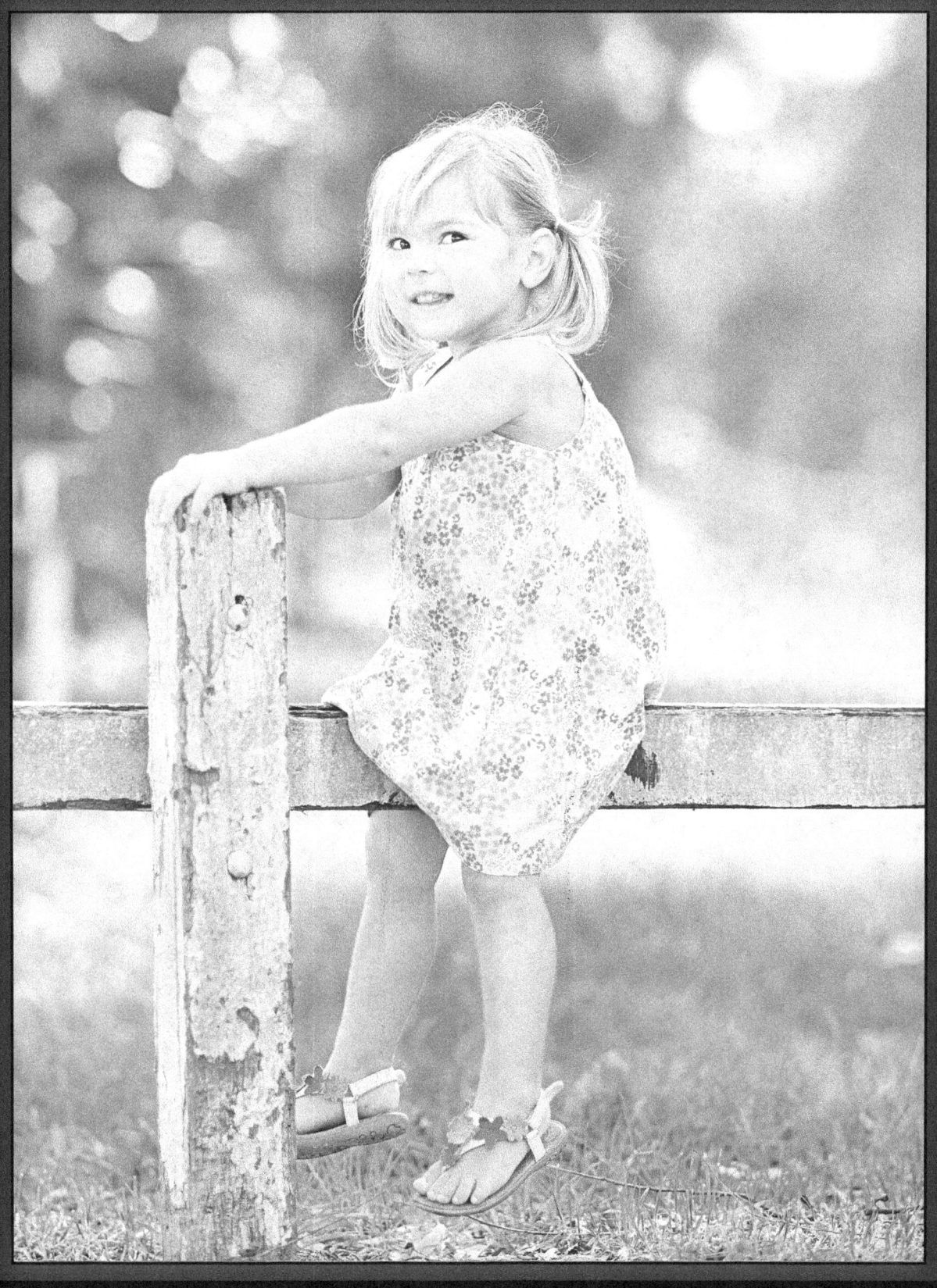

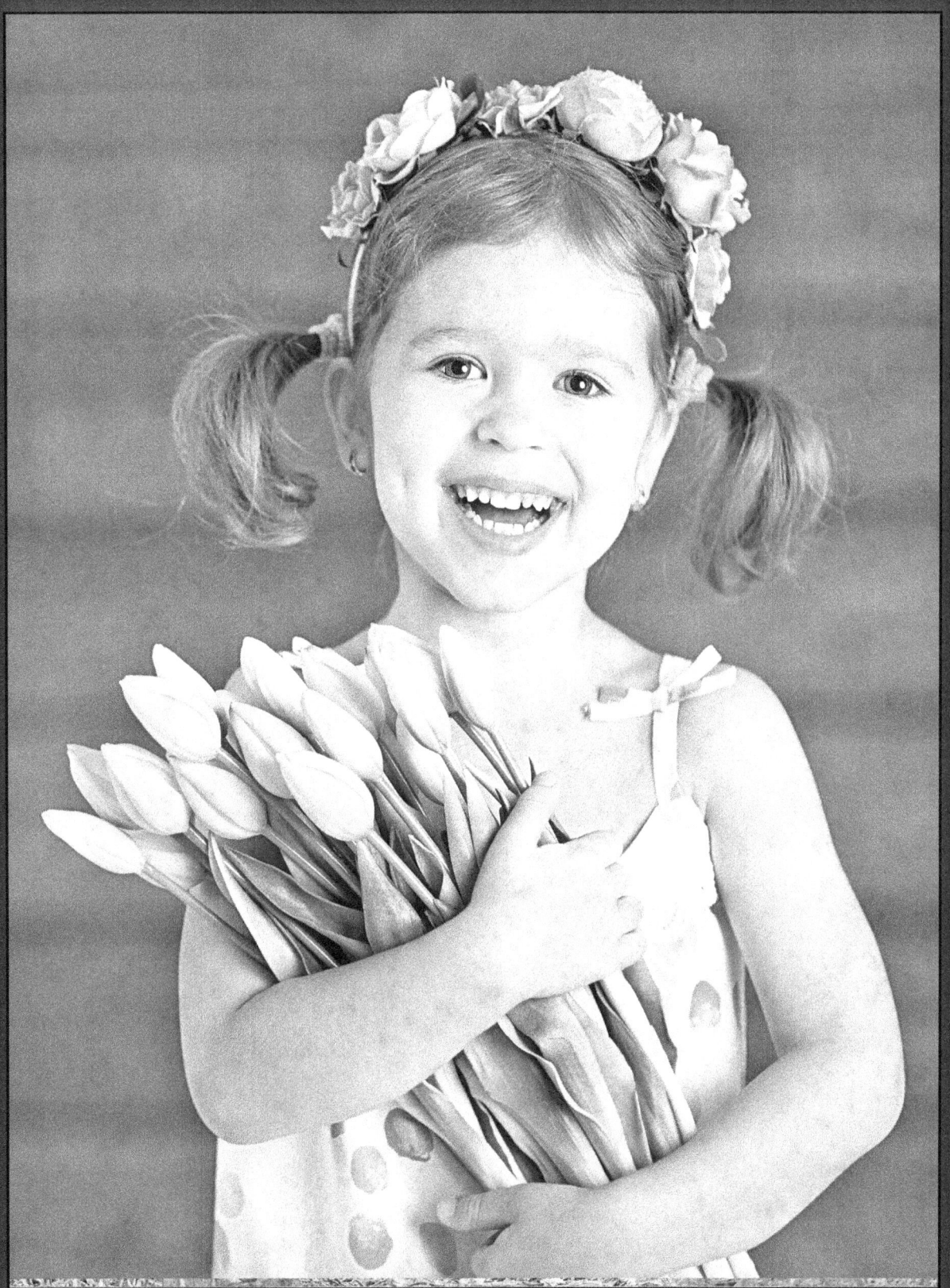

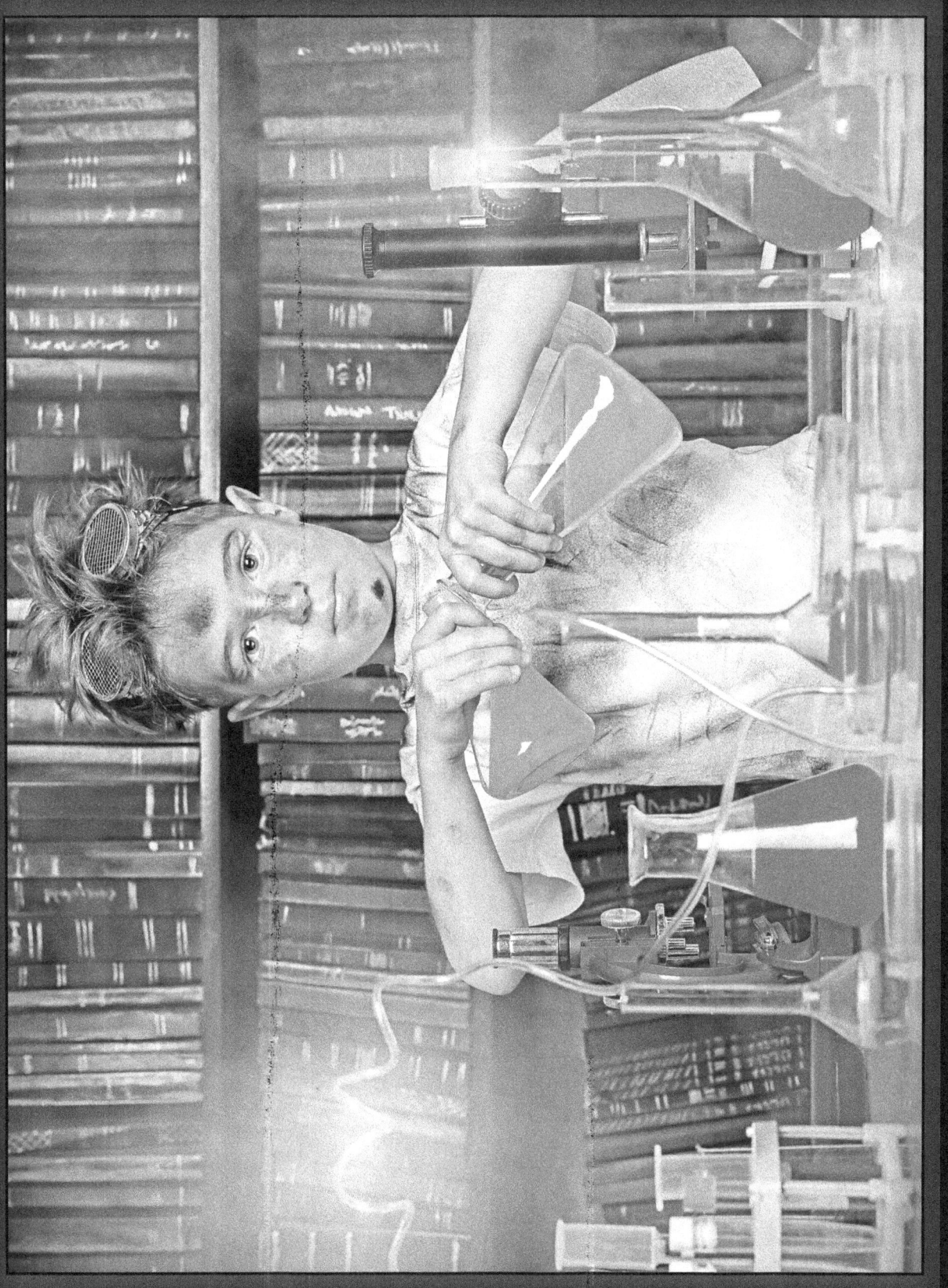

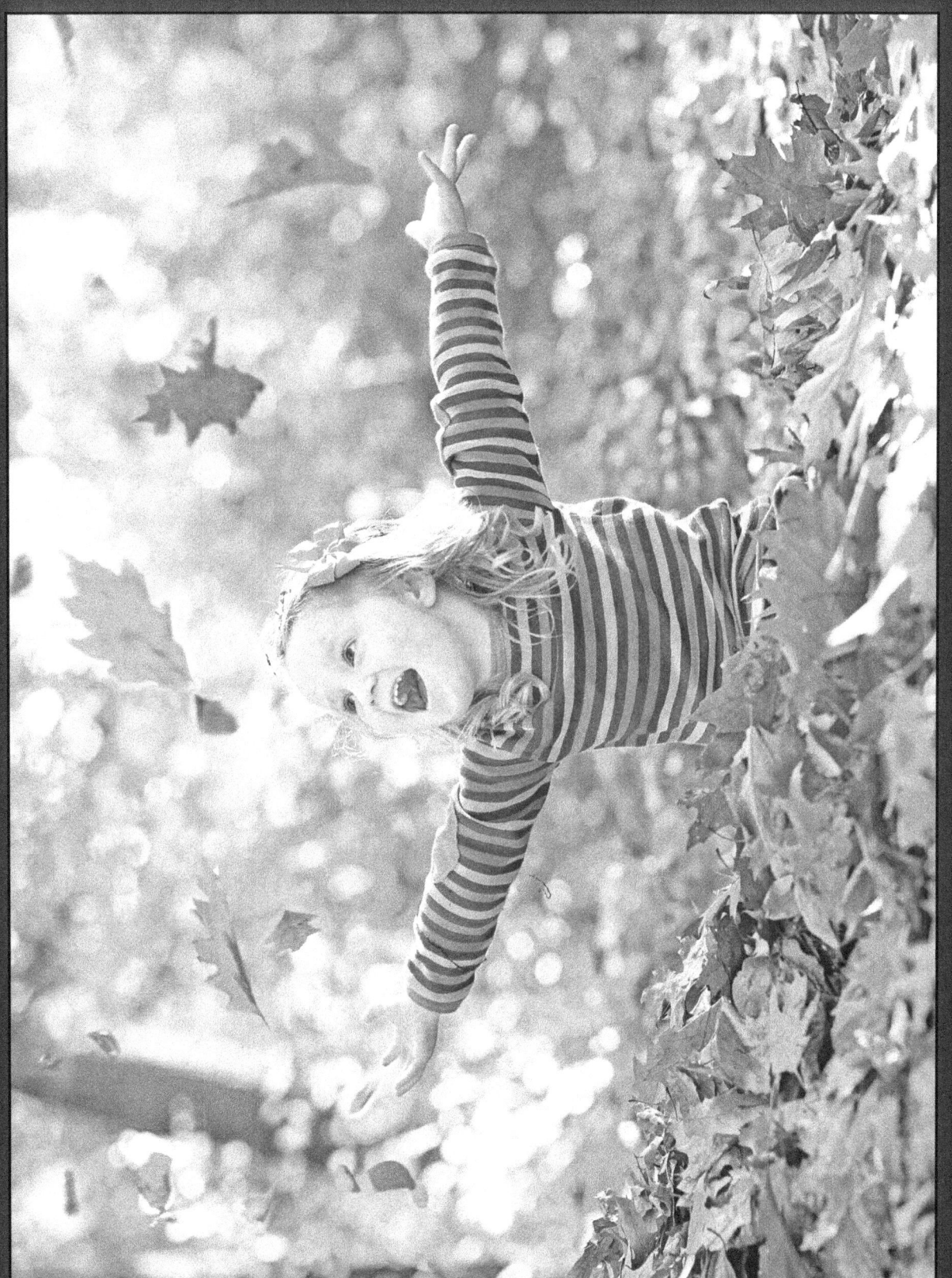

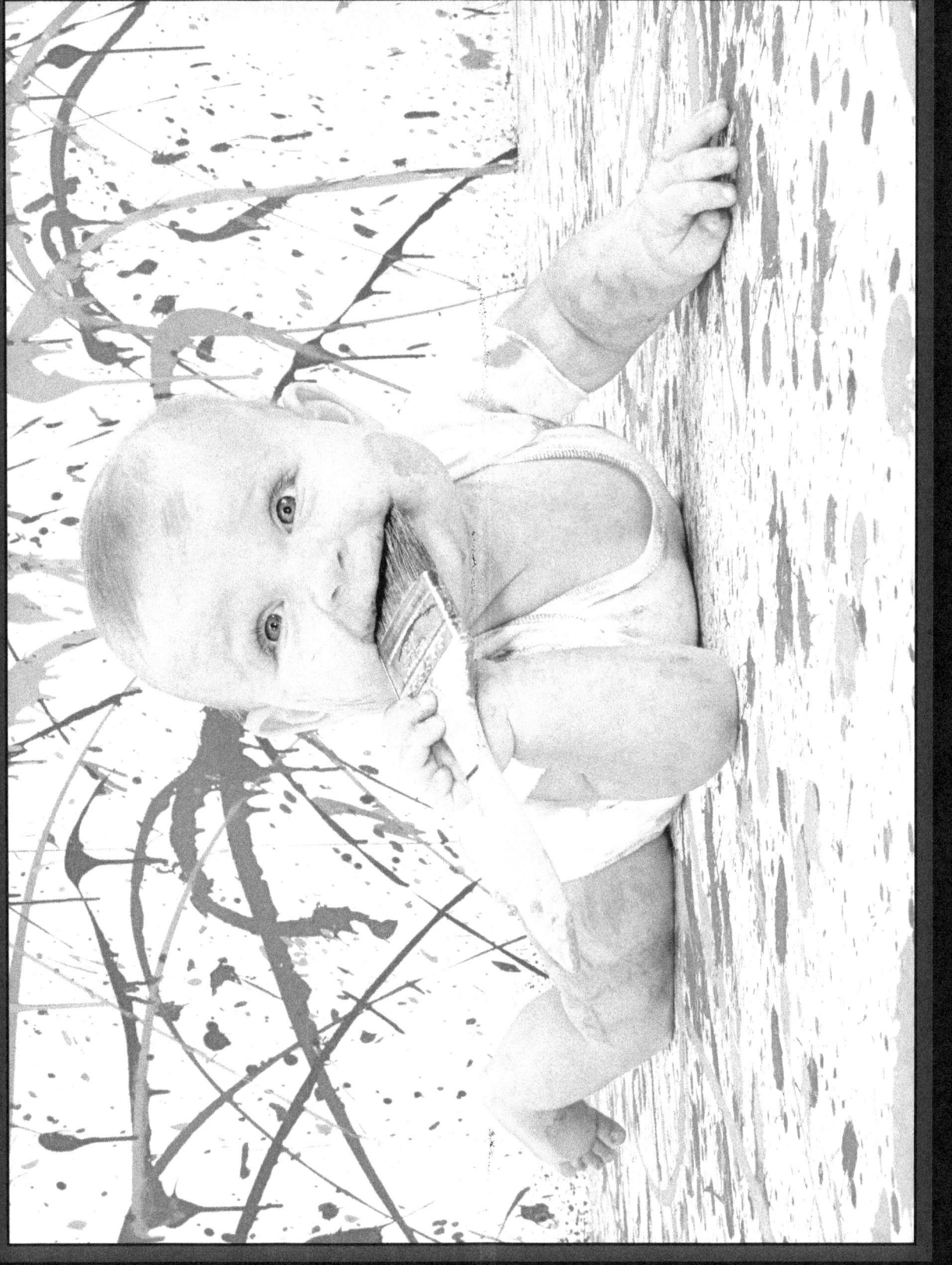

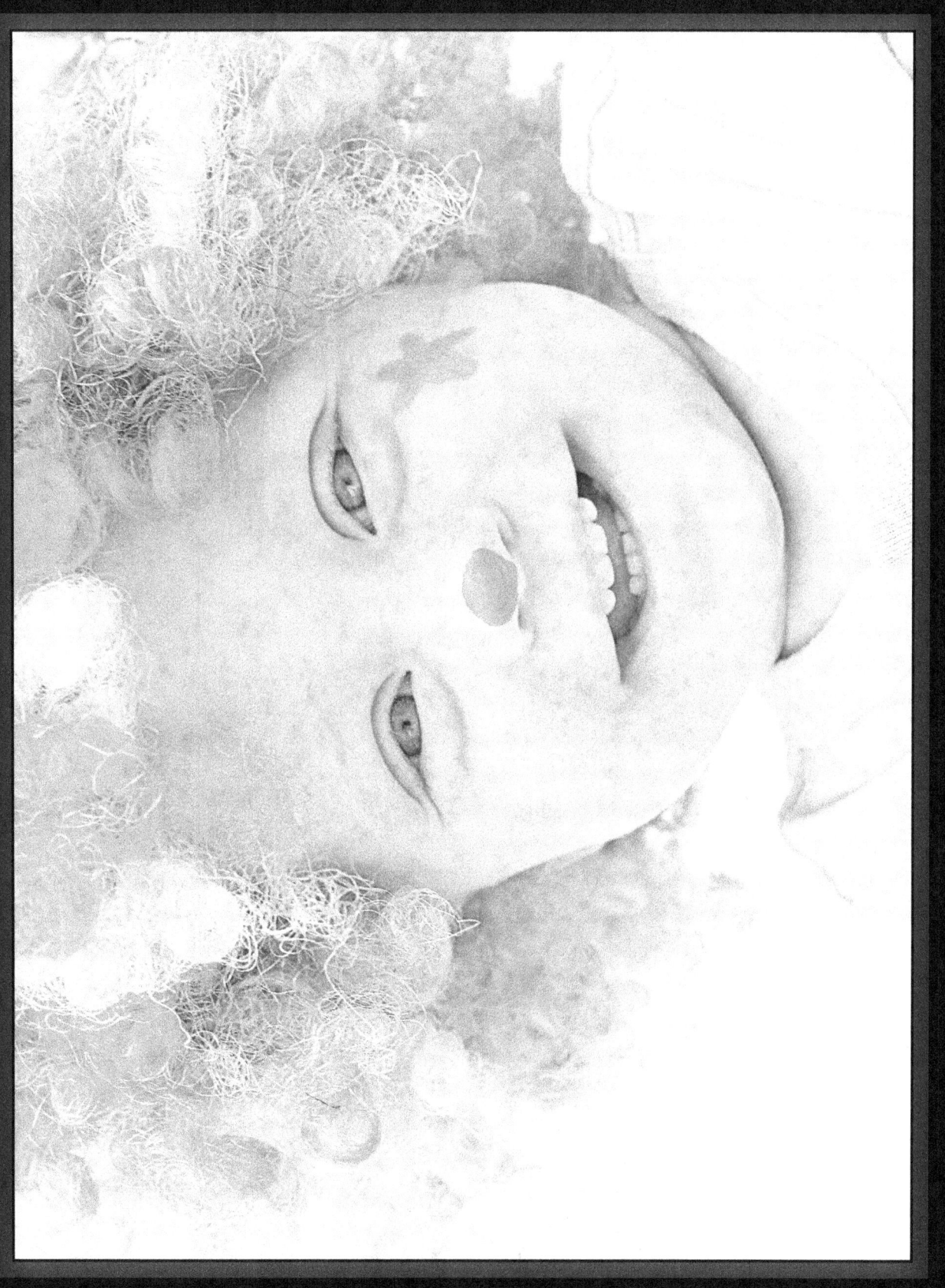

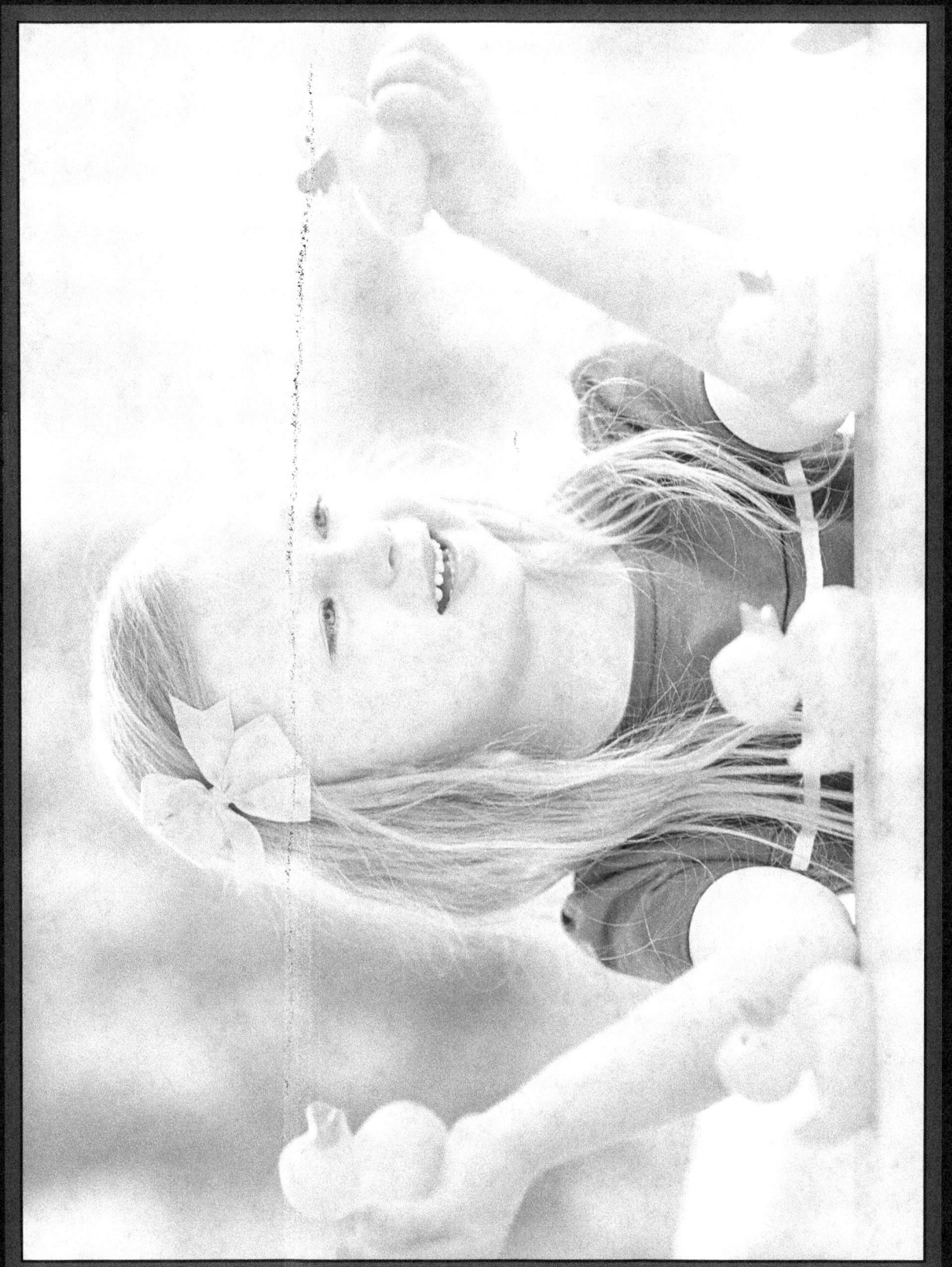

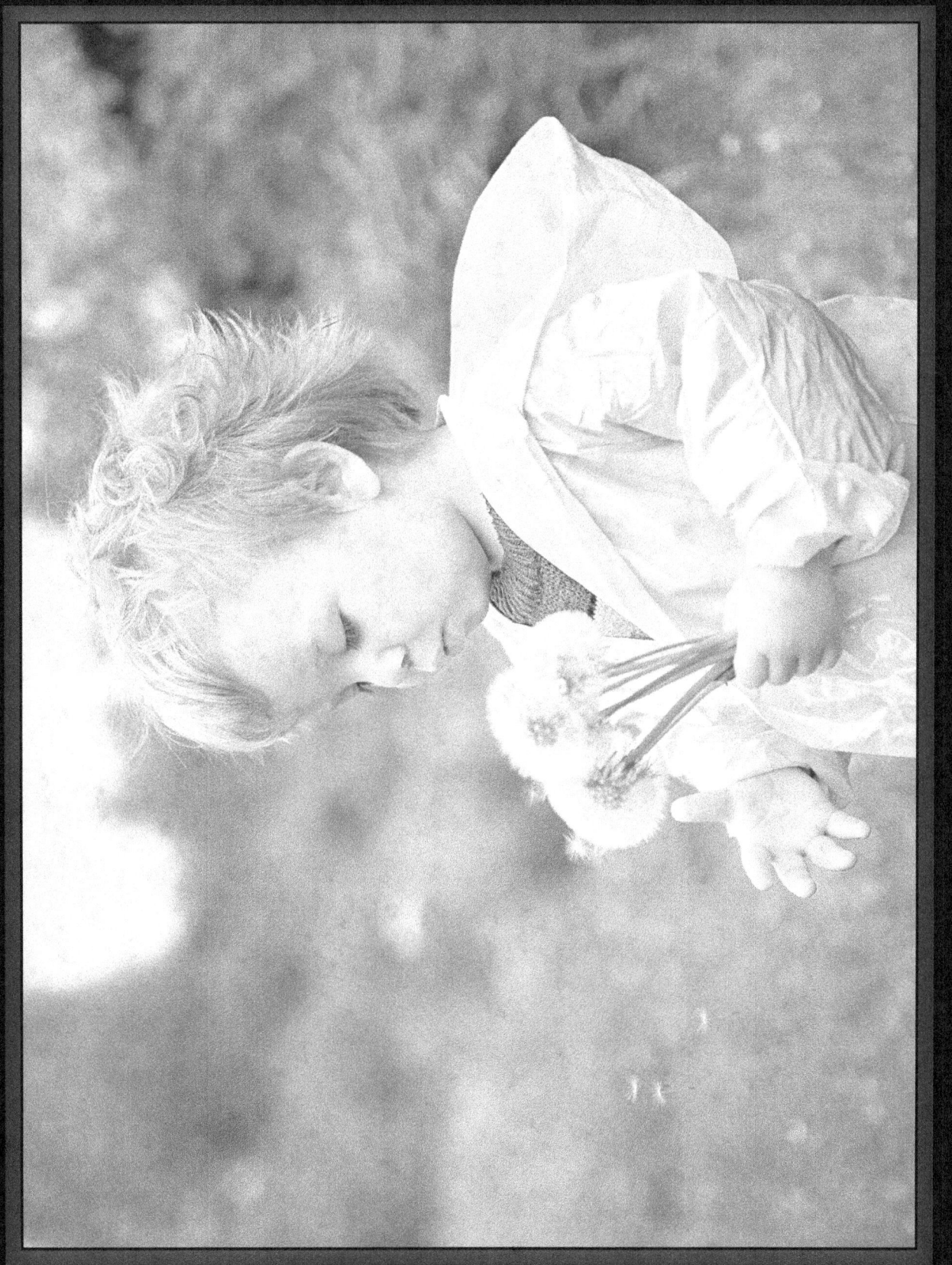

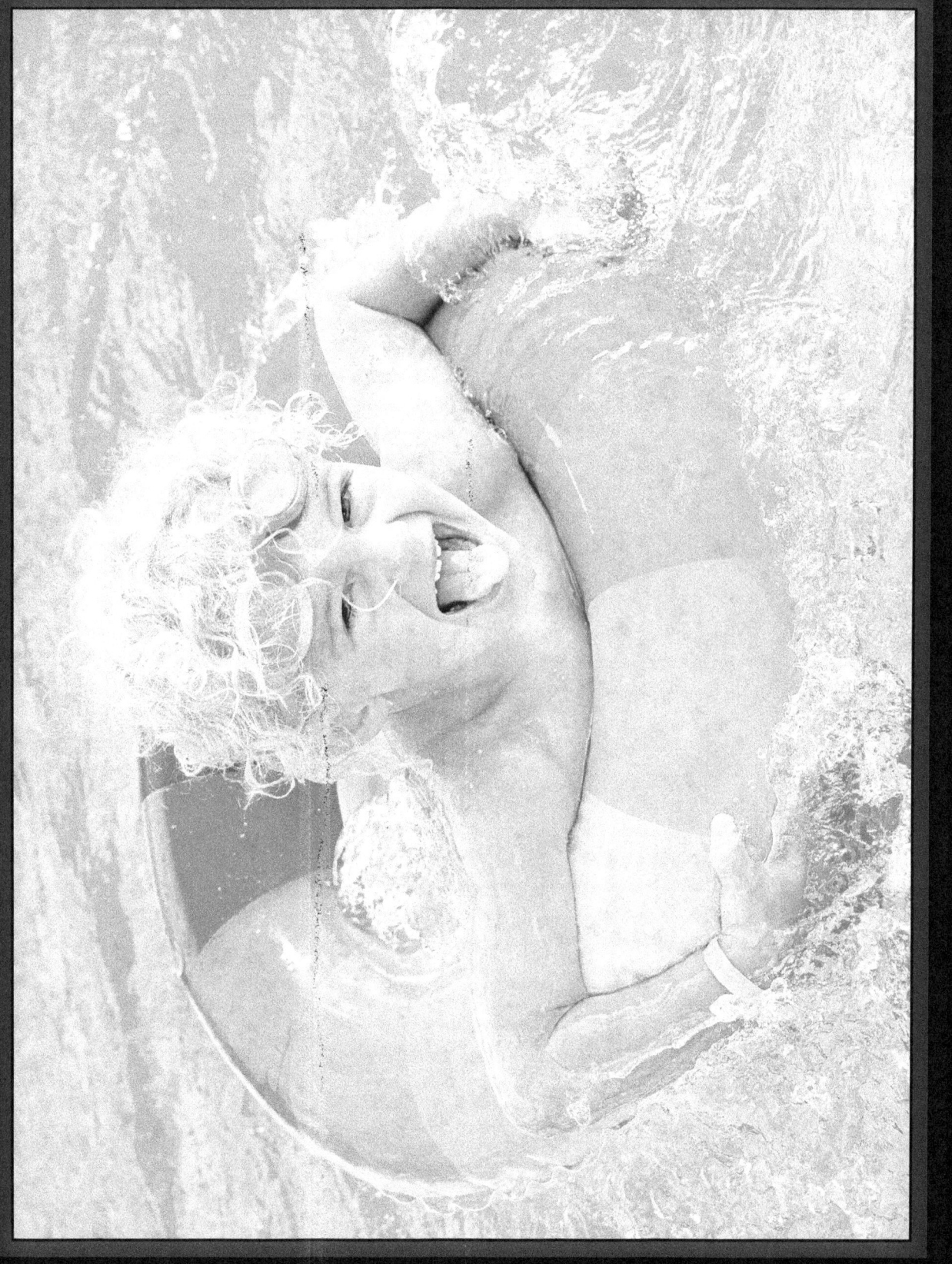

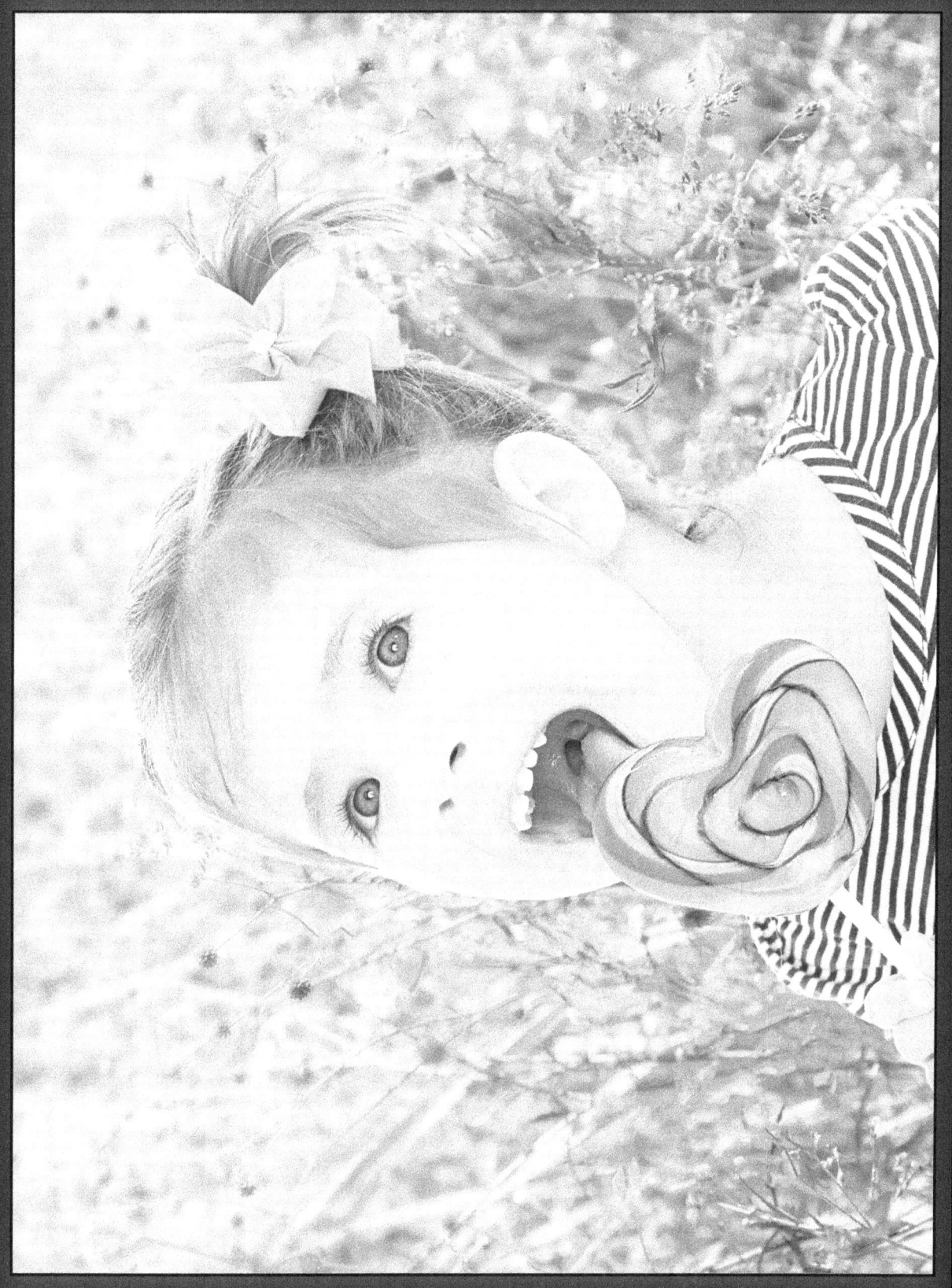

www.ingramcontent.com/pod-product-compliance
Lightning Source LLC
Chambersburg PA
CBHW081303180526
45170CB00007B/2547